D1616622

KIM DORLAND

KATERINA ATANASSOVA

ROBERT ENRIGHT

JEFFREY SPALDING

KIM DORLAND

Figure 1
Vancouver / Berkeley

McMichael Canadian Art Collection
Kleinburg, Ontario

Cataloguing data available from Library and Archives Canada
ISBN 978-1-927958-25-4 (hbk.)

Editing by Linda Pruessen
Copy editing by Judy Phillips
Design by Jessica Sullivan
Front cover: *You Are Here* (detail), Kim Dorland. Paul and Mary
Dailey Desmarais III, Montreal. Photo credit: Eden Robbins
Back cover: *Fuck Love* (detail), Kim Dorland. Collection Majudia,
Montreal. Photo credit: Eden Robbins
Printed and bound in Canada by Friesens
Distributed in the U.S. by Publishers Group West

Figure 1 Publishing Inc.
Vancouver BC Canada
www.figure1pub.com

McMichael Canadian Art Collection
Kleinburg ON Canada
www.mcmichael.com

THANK YOU

TO OUR SPONSORS AND DONORS FOR THEIR GENEROUS SUPPORT.

RBC EMERGING ARTISTS

ANGELL GALLERY

Anonymous in honour of Mary Dailey Pattee Desmarais and Paul Desmarais III

R. Brian Cartwright

Gail and W. Robert Farquharson

Megan Long

Petra and Lionel Newton

Neve Peric and Jim Balsillie

Belinda Stronach

CONTENTS

PREFACE

VICTORIA DICKENSON
EXECUTIVE DIRECTOR,
McMICHAEL CANADIAN
ART COLLECTION

WHEN THE EXHIBITION *You Are Here: Kim Dorland and the Return to Painting* opened in October 2013 at the McMichael Canadian Art Collection, it was evident that we were indeed in the presence of painting—great painting. There were wonderful works by Tom Thomson, David Milne, and members of the Group of Seven, for which the McMichael is well known, but it was the lashings of paint, the vibrant colours, and the singular vision of Kim Dorland that astounded the many visitors.

This book is a tribute to the energy and excitement that Kim has generated with his large, glowing canvases. Our thanks to the artist for his generosity in sharing his work through his exhibitions and now through this richly illustrated book. Our thanks as well to all the galleries and individuals who graciously lent their works for exhibition and for publication. Without the support of patrons like Robin Anthony at the Royal Bank of Canada, and Jamie Angell of the Angell Gallery in Toronto, and individual donors, this project would not have been possible. And we would be the poorer without the insights of those who have looked long and intently at Kim's work—Robert Enright, Jeff Spalding, and Katerina Atanassova, who first brought Kim to the McMichael with an inspired idea for an artist's residency. We are delighted to be able to bring one of Canada's most exciting painters to an even larger audience through this book.

The McMichael is dedicated to the collection and presentation of the works of artists who have made or are making a contribution to art in Canada. This publication is part of that mission.

FOREWORD

ROBIN ANTHONY
ART CURATOR, RBC

July 8, 1917 (Emma Lake series) 2009
oil and acrylic on wood panel, 60 × 96 in.

OVER THE PAST fifteen years, the Royal Bank of Canada (RBC) has identified and recognized more than two hundred emerging artists through the RBC Canadian Painting Competition. The competition is designed to identify painters in the early stages of their careers who show promise and dedication to their craft. Kim Dorland—a graduate of York University and the Emily Carr Institute of Art and Design— was one of those talented artists in 2006, and again in 2007. Since then, he has gone on to produce solo exhibitions in Canada and internationally, with several public art collections purchasing his work. It has been exciting to watch this competition alumnus's career grow.

RBC's interest in Dorland, and artists like him, stems from our desire to support artists early on in their careers by providing them with financing and opportunities for national visibility. Since the beginning of the painting competition, RBC has acquired more than forty works from finalists and winners, to be part of our corporate art collection. We've been fortunate to exhibit the finalists' artwork in many galleries across Canada, giving exposure to some of this country's finest up-and-coming painters.

As the curator of RBC's corporate art collection, I continue to watch the careers of these artists flourish as they grow professionally. It has been exciting to follow Kim Dorland's artistic growth. He is influenced and inspired by important Canadian artists such as Tom Thomson and the Group of Seven. The Canadian landscape has been a constant source of inspiration for artists, and I find it fascinating to see how Dorland interprets this tie to the landscape that so many of us experience. Also integral to Dorland's practice is his relationship with the people surrounding him. When I was initially introduced to Dorland's work, his themes centred on teenage activities in the streets and woods of Alberta. Since then, he has continued to work with depth and perspective in his landscapes. The volume and density of paint is expanding, and now we see it exploding off some canvases. In the more recent paintings, we are looking at Dorland's family and exploring how they interact. The urban and rural landscapes continue to be a source of inspiration, but the personalities are more evident in the portraits.

It is vital that we collectively continue to nurture national talent and ensure that audiences have access to these inspiring works. RBC is proud to support this publication and share the world we live in as seen through Dorland's eyes.

INTRODUCTION: GOING OUT ON A LIMB

JEFFREY SPALDING

IS ART DAMAGED? Is painting irreparably harmed? When you read the published preambles to the discussions of Kim Dorland's art, you might very well get the impression that we accept that painting is a goner. Kim Dorland didn't get the memo.

Dorland makes exquisitely ugly paintings. Achingly poignant, touching, melancholic but ever so vital, his work is a study in contradictions and contrasts: beauty and defilement, exhilaration and denouement, elegance and the tawdry, happiness and despondency. He is fanatically dedicated, making an astonishing number of works in a variety of media and scales. He ransacks art history, exploring almost every theme and subject. And he is tireless in his pursuit of pushing the limits of his own taste. Someone forgot to tell him that it is all over, finished. Thankfully.

Recently, the artist concluded a residency with the McMichael Canadian Art Collection that resulted in an exhibition pitting his work alongside Group of Seven works from its collection. Clearly, it was a triumph, with the exuberant Dorland works of grand scale playing off against the intimate sketches of the Group: *Hot Mush School 2014*. Harris, Thomson, and Milne were all "quoted" by his responses. Tellingly, Dorland responded to the post-impressionistic work of the Group—that is, the Group's style before its dramatic stylistic turnaround in 1921 in response to "the call to order." Dorland's lush impasto excesses result in works of great power; many of these could be termed true homages to this legacy. In this respect, these works in combination with his Emma Lake pictures provide an adoring embrace, a sweeping emotional endorsement of the power of art to move us and uplift our spirit. His paintings that capture the artist, easel, and painting set amidst the trees are so touching—a closing of the circle, an extraordinary gesture of respect from one generation to another. They are powerful, iconic, and so convincing that it is possible to cast these as prototypical, signature-style Dorland works.

Yet they career us off the centre of where Dorland lives. He doesn't seem to believe in the redemptive power of nature, the

Ghost of a Drunk (or Self Portrait) 2013
oil and acrylic on jute, 96 × 72 in.

theosophical underpinning of the Group's commitment. Perhaps Dorland sees nature, life, or spirit as damaged? Kim Dorland's art is inhabited by ghosts. Many of his works wrestle with the demons of his past life, reflections upon uncomfortable, bumpy teen years and early manhood spent in Alberta. Kicked out of the house as a teenager, estranged from his parents, without home or emotional rudder, he was saved by art and Lori Seymour. Seemingly, he wishes to repay the debt by saving art through countless painterly tributes to his muse—his spouse, Lori—as well as to his children.

In the mid-1950s, Graham Coughtry would speak for the aspirations of the art of a new generation by infamously exclaiming that "every damn tree in the country has been painted." Working today, Kim Dorland's art observes that "every damn tree in the country has been painted upon." It may still be plausible to manufacture an encounter with pristine wilderness, but it is not our predominant, day-to-day lived reality. Instead, we learn to endure urban gardens strewn with debris and dog feces, buildings and trees "tagged" by graffiti artists, posters, and advertisements.

Great city "green spaces" are also the scene for many indecent, lewd acts. Much of Dorland's art visits this aspect of nature. A nearby forest retreat is not an oasis and source of spiritual release but a place for the disenfranchised to come together, inhabit, and somewhat own—a teenage universe. His bush party paintings remember his high-school years in Alberta, drinking, fighting, or one's "first time" in the backseat of an old beater or under a railway bridge. In so many ways, the sentiments captured by these paintings are painful, despondent, and so very dreadful. Yet they are real. They reflect the lived experience of legions of youth: cue Kurt Cobain, and Isabella Rossellini in the movie *Blue Velvet*. So perhaps we must smile and accept. Dorland's paintings move me.

Kim Dorland has been exceedingly forthcoming and generous in his expression of admiration for and emulation of several powerful artistic influences. A certain number of them are recounted in every published account, so I won't recite herein.

▲ *First Time* 2006
oil, acrylic, and spray paint on canvas over wood panel, 36 × 30 in.

▶ *36 Olympic Green* 2007
oil, acrylic, and spray paint on canvas over wood panel, 72 × 96 in.

Fuck Love 2008
oil, acrylic, spray paint, ink, and screws on wood panel, 72 × 96 in.

Wooded Area 2006
oil and acrylic on canvas over wood panel, 96 × 96 in.

To be honest, it is probably because I don't actually feel these "grand" references are all that pertinent to a discussion of his work. Instead, I perhaps take a different view. I wonder whether much of Dorland's temperament was honed in the west, in Alberta?

Whereas much of the twentieth-century art of eastern Canada might have been about beauty and extraordinary views, art in western Canada tended to be far more prosaic, understated, pedestrian. Dorothy Knowles, A.C. Leighton, Walter Phillips, Jim Nicoll, and so many more made paintings of vernacular, down-to-earth, everyday reality. Wilf Perreault has made a career out of painting muddy backstreet residential alleyways; David Thauberger has chronicled the wartime suburban houses of his hometown; photographer Danny Singer looks at main street small-town Alberta. Dorland's "portraits" of trailers, trampolines, teens, and suburban houses reside within this tradition. All choose to record the ordinary, the mundane, in preference to the exemplary. Dorland adds further pathos—empty beer cans, starving dogs, dilapidated cars, spray-bombed fences, strip-mall convenience stores, trailer park boys—diminishing expectations. Why am I not totally depressed by these works? Do I even like, never mind love, these paintings? I suppose I do, because they strive to tell the truth. Dorland's art declares: *This is our reality; this is what we have come to.*

Kim Dorland's figuration and landscapes sit as a continuity of Canadian art history, not as an anomaly. Institutional authority may undervalue the likes of Joanne Tod, Paterson Ewen, W.L. Stevenson, Maxwell Bates, Michael Smith, Landon Mackenzie, Arthur Lismer, Goodridge Roberts, John Hartman, Doug Kirton, Harold Klunder, William Ronald, Claude Breeze, Jean-Paul Riopelle. Should we mention Karel Appel and CoBrA? I can assure you, given Dorland's voracious interest in art, he does not. His work is so evidently mindful of the glories of other beloved art.

Kim Dorland has created some of the most aggressive, awful paintings. Their malaise hurts; some make me very sad. He has "tagged" art history: *I'm awfully glad.*

▲▲ Sterling Road studio, Toronto, 2009

▲ Sterling Road studio, Toronto, 2009

► *Ozzy* 2006
oil, acrylic, and spray paint on linen over wood panel, 30 × 36 in.

The Loner 2005
acrylic on canvas, 84 × 60 in.

▲ *Crossing Elk* 2006
oil, acrylic, and spray paint on linen
over wood panel, 60 × 48 in.

▶ *New Father* 2006
oil and acrylic on canvas over
wood panel, 36 × 30 in.

▲ *Fire Pit* 2006
  oil and acrylic on canvas, 24 × 20 in.

▶ *Wooded Area (2nd View)* 2006
  oil and acrylic on canvas over wood
  panel, 60 × 48 in.

▲ *Her* 2007
oil on canvas over wood panel,
72 × 60 in.

▶ *Her #6* 2006
oil, acrylic, spray paint and screws on
wood panel, 96 × 72 in.

Dead End 2007
oil, acrylic, and spray paint on wood panel, 96 × 144 in.

Northern Lights 2007
oil and acrylic on canvas, 72 × 96 in.

Woods 2007
oil, acrylic, and spray paint on canvas, 72 × 96 in.

Catwalk 2007
oil and acrylic on canvas, 24 × 30 in.

▲ *Her Favourite Place* 2007
oil, acrylic, and spray paint on canvas,
48 × 60 in.

▶ *Trampoline* 2007
oil, acrylic, and spray paint on canvas
over wood panel, 48 × 60 in.

Lake Louise 2008
oil and acrylic on wood panel, 60 × 48 in.

▲ *Red Bronco* 2008
oil, acrylic, and spray paint on
wood panel, 16 × 20 in.

▶ *Sled* 2008
oil and acrylic on wood panel,
60 × 48 in.

▲ *Lori in a Blue Shirt* 2008
oil and spray paint on wood panel,
72 × 72 in.

▶ *Untitled (Lavender Lori)* 2008
oil and spray paint on wood panel,
20 × 16 in.

▲ *Nature Painting* 2008
  oil, acrylic, and spray paint on canvas,
  60 × 72 in.

▶ *Nature Painting #2* 2008
  oil and acrylic on wood panel,
  72 × 96 in.

Parking Lot Conversation #2 2009
oil and acrylic on wood panel, 72 × 96 in.

▲ *Kiss* 2009
oil on wood panel, 72 × 60 in.

▶ *Twilight* 2009
oil on wood panel, 72 × 60 in.

36

▲ *R.I.P. Tom Thomson* 2009
oil, acrylic, ink, and stickers on wood
panel, 96 × 72 in.

▶ *Woods #6* 2009
oil, acrylic, spray paint, ink, paper and
screws on wood panel, 144 × 192 in.

▲ *Sasquatch* 2009
oil and fur on wood panel, 96 × 72 in.

▶ *Angel of Death* 2009
oil and acrylic on wood panel, 72 × 96 in.

YOU ARE HERE: KIM DORLAND AND THE RETURN TO PAINTING

KATERINA ATANASSOVA

You Are Here: Kim Dorland and the Return to Painting ran at the McMichael Canadian Art Collection from October 26, 2013, to January 5, 2014. Curated by Katerina Atanassova, the critically acclaimed exhibition paid homage to a century-old tradition of landscape painting as seen through the eyes of a young Canadian artist. It also sparked an immediate discussion on the subject of looking at nature.[1]

AT THE TURN of the nineteenth century, trekking remote areas in search of opportunities to record exhilarating art experiences was hugely popular, in both Europe and North America. But with the advent of urban life and modern abstract painting, that practice became little more than a pastime.[2] In recent years, however, we are witnessing a slow yet steady resurgence of this once-popular trend—a re-embracing of nature as a source of inspiration, in terms of both its public presence and its appeal to young artists. Kim Dorland is at the forefront of a younger generation of artists whose work has contributed greatly to the renewed power of painting in the landscape.

The exhibition *You Are Here: Kim Dorland and the Return to Painting* was born out of an intriguing idea: to introduce the work of a contemporary artist while simultaneously paying homage to a century-old tradition of landscape painting in Canada. The majority of the small sketches and large panoramic views of untamed landscapes included in the exhibition were created during the artist-in-residence program at the McMichael Canadian Art Collection in Kleinburg, Ontario, in the summer months of 2013. As plans for the exhibition progressed, Kim and I trekked around the gallery's hundred-acre grounds in search of inspiring subjects. As we walked—Kim photographing the woods with an old Polaroid camera, and both of us watching the long-expired film translate the greenery into variations of sepia—it became obvious that a dialogue with works from the McMichael's permanent collection would form the backbone of the installation.

A careful selection of historical works from the gallery's collection gave Kim the freedom to go back to his studio and respond to specific subject matter, to play with elements of composition or even technical subtleties akin to his own artistic pursuits. The exhibition opened in October 2013 and immediately brought about a discussion on the subject of looking at nature. What began as strictly an artist-curator dialogue had moved to the public sphere, and called for a renewed interest in the Canadian

You Are Here 2013
oil and acrylic on jute over wood panel, 20 × 16 in.

wilderness. At the same time, it also demanded an examination of human relationships with nature and an exploration of a sense of place and identity within the context of uniquely Canadian experiences.

Inspired by artists such as Tom Thomson (1877–1917), Emily Carr (1871–1945), David Milne (1882–1953), and selected members of the Group of Seven—and their quest for bold, authentic, and expressive visual language—the Alberta-born Dorland not only celebrates the importance of nature in his work but also addresses the essential question of the artist as a creator within nature. In *You Are Here* (P. 42), he uses the dark outline of his figure standing in front of an easel and facing a flashing red canvas to highlight his personal response to the true northern character of his native land. How are we, the viewers, to associate with that image of the artist immersed in a dark, almost menacing woodland? Is this a nostalgic return to nature, or an uncomfortable premonition of our not-so-distant future when, suffocated by the claustrophobia of our modern existence, we too seek a deep wild forest where we can recharge?

The artists who trail-blazed in search of an authentic and original interpretation of the Canadian landscape have long inspired Dorland's imagination. As a teenager, confronting his first desires to paint, Kim came rather by accident upon illustrations of Tom Thomson and the Group of Seven's works in Peter Mullen's comprehensive study of their origins and rise to fame.[3] Like many Canadians, he felt an instant connection to their works and their nationalistic sense of pride and identity with their homeland. Such connection gave birth to a singular ambition: "Before I found art, I had no sense of the future. I could have ended up in a dead-end job or even jail, not because I was violent but because I was thoughtless. Then I found this. It is all I wanted."[4] This ambition, Kim believes, led to a search for his own sense of belonging through expression in art.

Can up-close study of the bold Thomson sketches and rapid brushwork substitute for first lessons in painting? Can

▲ Preparing for the McMichael, Dufferin Street studio, Toronto, 2013

▶ *You Are Here*, exhibition view, McMichael Canadian Art Collection, Kleinburg, Ontario, 2013

44

examination of the colour sense of Fred Varley (1881–1969) be an introduction to colour theory? Or can an exploration of the treatment of surface by J.E.H. MacDonald (1873–1932) serve as a first demonstration in application of paint on a canvas? Such speculations are for future researchers to debate, yet one thing is certain: from the start, a fire was lit in the young artist's heart, sparking an urge to pick up the brush and explore his own expressive abilities. The more he looked and absorbed the Group's visual language, the more confident and determined he became in his own ability to apply form and texture and to relate a specific subject through representation or abstraction in paint. "My work," Dorland asserts, "is very much about paint. It's about other things too: landscape, portraiture, identity, psychology… but for me, it always comes back to the medium."

Unlike other artists of his generation, Dorland made a conscious choice to work in the old traditions of oil painting, which rather than intimidating him was always a source of inspiration, and he never lost faith in the centuries-old medium and its ability to communicate with the viewer. His novel approach to the medium is expressed in his characteristic and uniquely multi-layered impasto, rendered with a vigour and density never seen before. For contemporary audiences, the physicality of the paint combines with the social context, erupting in pointed and poignant questioning of our evolving relationship with our surroundings, physical and psychological.

Thomson's sketches (for example, *The Tent*, (P. 47)) betray an intimate familiarity with place that fosters a sense of authentic human attachment and feeling of belonging. At the turn of the nineteenth century, the sense of discovery welcomed the viewer into a different universe: peaceful, harmonious, and inviting. Thomson acted not only as an artist but also as a generous host, as a guide, as a ranger. It is not surprising that the campsites, lakes, rivers, and waterfalls of his beloved Algonquin Park, familiar to him from numerous trips, provided a strong sense of identity—a

▲ Painting on the French River, 2013

▶ **Tom Thomson,** *The Tent* 1915
oil on wood panel, 8½ × 10½ in.

Canadian identity deeply felt by the people connected to that environment. Although the work itself lacks human presence, the sense of place in Thomson's work depends on human existence; it is we who give meaning to that vast, undifferentiated space.

Thomson's focus on the wide, untamed landscape of northern Ontario, as in *Woodland Waterfall* (P. 62), led him to investigate weather in all its changing aspects—from season to season, from day to night, from calm to sudden storms. His ability to record these changes in an artistic form allowed him to render the mood and poetry of the northern wilderness through the intense personal nature of his sketches.

Artists such as Thomson were often experienced guides and canoeists who knew how to set up a camp and survive in remote locations. Each year, they travelled long distances in search of new subjects to paint. Yet the wild offered more than just beautiful scenery and visually fulfilling experiences to these adventurous souls. Each trip into the Canadian wilderness left a deep and lasting spiritual impression and stimulated a connection to the land that they had never before experienced. Expressing his agitations of the soul to his patron Dr. MacCallum, Thomson wrote, "The best I can do does not do the place much justice in the way of beauty."[5] Singularly responsible for introducing the iconography of the lone tree as a metaphor in Canadian art, Thomson, through his art, had and continues to have a powerful symbolic resonance for artists working today, as can be appreciated in Dorland's *Green Tree, Blue Tree #2* (P. 49), which echoes the immediacy of Thomson's *Wood Interior, Winter* (P. 50).

David Milne, on the other hand, showed a strong interest in making an autonomous picture that worked by its own standards, rather than faithfully rendering the scene. His highly individual idiom was stimulated by studying the forms he found in nature, but in contrast to the landscape studies of Thomson and his contemporaries, Milne's work appears far more abstract. In *Painting Place: Brown and Black* (P. 51), Milne's sense of place was "tempered" by his sense of pictorial order.[6] To him, understanding

Green Tree, Blue Tree #2 2009
oil, acrylic, and spray paint on wood panel, 60 × 60 in.

Tom Thomson, *Wood Interior, Winter* 1916
oil on wood panel, 8½ × 26½ in.

David Milne, *Painting Place: Brown and Black* c. 1926
oil on canvas, 12 × 16 in.

how a sense of place develops and changes is relevant to understanding how people interact with their close surroundings.

At least three generations later, Dorland's fresh contemporary work is instantly recognizable not only by the heavy impasto and the preference for neon-bright colours but also by its different assertion of the human presence in nature. As modern urban dwellers, we often feel awkward in the woods; we know not where we belong. Is it truly the primordial forest or is it part of our childhood imaginary world (the wild we learned about through fairy tales)? Subconsciously, childhood experiences can drive the need to make sense of place and to search out familiar surroundings. When speaking of the unique bond that develops between children and their childhood environments, sociologists often refer to the "primal landscape."

In *New Home* (P. 53), Dorland's grandfather's trailer is perched on the outskirts of town. Bright colours mask its shabby appearance, yet its remoteness speaks of someone who seeks isolation from the urban reality. There is a combined sense of mystery and human tragedy. The image of the lonely trailer suggests a voluntary or forced alienation, an attempt to escape from one's reality into the dream world of the enchanted forest. Dorland's world— although referencing locales in his native Wainwright, Alberta— is no longer focused on a specific place but rather represents a kind of "anywhere." The trailer, so often associated with homelessness and social instability, could itself be anywhere—in the slums of a major industrial city or on the outskirts of a provincial town. It is not the trailer but its occupant who creates the subtext, and the image we are left with is not of the happy camper vacationing briefly in a tent.

This novel way of positioning nature is further explored in *Northern Lights* (P. 55). Here, Dorland introduces the lonesome lovers seated on the shore of Waskesiu Lake, absorbed in the mysterious spectacle of the northern lights. A sense of permanence and grandeur permeates the scene. There are obvious elements of staging in this composition that remind us of the

New Home 2006
oil and acrylic on canvas over wood panel, 60 × 48 in.

▲ Tom Thomson, *Moonlight and Birches* 1915
oil on wood panel, 8½ × 10½ in.

▶ *Northern Lights* 2007
oil and acrylic on canvas over wood panel, 60 × 72 in.

artist's overall control of his environment. The two strategically placed figures appear in the lower right-hand corner; on the left is the heavy, almost sculptural presence of the black tree to balance the composition. There is a tension between order and disorder at the heart of this haunting nocturnal scene. In contrast to the calm and sparkling *Moonlight and Birches* (P. 54), Dorland's *Northern Lights* captures a beauty created by the forces of opposition.

A similar contrast between unease and peaceful harmony is observed in Dorland's *Lost Mother #2* (P. 57), with its heavy impasto and its forlorn figures looking into a snowy landscape, contrasted with, for example, the A.Y. Jackson *Early Spring, Emileville, Quebec* (P. 58). Nature is imbued with a psychological undertone that sets up an intense psychological dialogue between artist and viewers. In Dorland's work, the forest often seems to be closing in on the artist, neither inviting nor foreboding, but pervaded by a feeling of intensity and danger. The dark outlines and the rendering of positive and negative space remind us of David Milne's *Side Door, Clarke's House* (P. 59).

Dorland's nature-inspired works are usually developed over a period, often beginning with field trips and Polaroid photo documentation, and sometimes drawn from remote and wild areas in his native Alberta. In his large-scale compositions, he neither broadens nor abbreviates the view. Instead, he often zooms in on the immediate surroundings and opens a veil in them for himself. That window of self-representation, portrayed as the artist at work—caught in a moment of complete immersion and unity with nature—is the breakthrough from the beautiful, impenetrable landscape to a place of one's own. The irony in such staging is that Dorland himself is not an *en plein air* artist and prefers the comfort of his studio to painting outdoors. His preference for large-scale compositions such as *Dripping Dream* (P. 61) could not be indulged during an outdoor painting adventure, like those typical for the artists from the turn of the nineteenth century.[7] Despite their large scale, Dorland's forest landscapes lend themselves to

▲ With kids at the Dufferin Street studio, Toronto, 2012

▶ *Lost Mother #2* 2011
  oil and acrylic on jute, 72 × 96 in.

A.Y. Jackson, *Early Spring, Emileville, Quebec* 1913
oil on canvas, 25 × 32½ in.

David Milne, *Side Door, Clarke's House*   c. 1923
oil on canvas, 12 × 16 in.

Dripping Dream 2013
oil and acrylic on jute, 72 × 96 in.

a simple reduction of forms. Nature is stripped down to the bare essentials: line, shape, and colour. In *Woodland Waterfall* (P. 62), one of the historical works Kim chose to respond to, Thomson used stylized tree branches and flat areas of strong colour. In *Woodland Waterfall (after Tom Thomson)* (P. 63), Dorland systematically dissected and recreated the composition.

Thomson also appears as a subject in some of Dorland's works, many of which explore his mythological presence in Canadian art. *The Painter in His Canoe* (P. 64) creates a narrative associated with the boisterous life of this bohemian artist in the wild, living carefree, fishing, canoeing, trekking, all while devoting his life to painting. *Seconds Before* (P. 65) evokes a sense of premonition. The use of vibrant red electrifies the canvas, making us shiver with the knowledge that a tragedy is about to happen, but forcing us to find some humour in it. Dorland plays with the mythology by turning a mysterious story into an uncomplicated tragic accident.

The image of the Canadian primal forest has been a magnetic visual experience and a daring adventure for generations of artists whose sensitive nature has allowed them to respond more acutely to their surroundings. In the first decades of the nineteenth century, better-equipped modern artists acquired the skills necessary to endure the extreme weather conditions and harsh grip of the northern country—skills they packed along with their painting gear. The images of western Canada, known for their whimsical energy and intricate play with light—such as in Emily Carr's *British Columbia Forest* (P. 66)—speak to the same electrifying charge evident in Dorland's *Untitled (Heavy Beams)* (P. 67). The work was included in the series *Enter, Light* from the fall of 2011. As if to signify an advent of new impulses, the beams of light charge the surface and signal the artist's emergence from a period of darkness into a new world, warm, bright, and welcoming. The forest is no longer a place of danger and menace. The web of encroaching, threatening branches is broken, and the beams of light are the forerunners of change and awakening.

▲ **Tom Thomson,** *Woodland Waterfall* 1916–17
oil on canvas, 48 × 52 in.

▶ *Woodland Waterfall (after Tom Thomson)* 2013
oil, acrylic, and spray paint on canvas over wood panel, 72 × 96 in.

▲ *The Painter in His Canoe* 2013
  oil and acrylic on jute over wood panel,
  72 × 96 in.

▶ *Seconds Before* 2009
  oil on canvas, 24 × 30 in.

▲ **Emily Carr,** *British Columbia Forest* c. 1930
oil on paper adhered to stretched canvas,
36 × 24 in.

▶ *Untitled (Heavy Beams)* 2011
oil on canvas, 60 × 48 in.

French River 2013
oil and acrylic on jute over wood panels, 96 × 216 in.

The works painted during Dorland's residency at the McMichael Canadian Art Collection in response to works from the permanent collection helped focus his personal quest toward understanding nature. "Working on this project with the McMichael," Dorland explains, "I was struck by how much has changed since the time of the Group, but also how little. Canadians are still drawn to that need to contemplate and articulate this gnarly wilderness that surrounds us. And painting—which has 'died' and come back to life multiple times even in my short career—still resonates. David Milne's paintings are still exceptional. A Thomson still 'works' in a contemporary context. The McMichael Collection is still very relevant. As a painter and a fan of painting—and a Thomson fanatic—that's a very exciting thing."[8]

These paintings also created a fresh way to engage younger audiences with the McMichael's historical collection.[9] Particular attention was given to the creation of the large triptych *French River* (P. 68–69). Despite the nearly one hundred years' distance, Dorland's works share a spirit and painterly execution characteristic of the works of Thomson, Carr, Milne, and the members of the Group. The inclusion of "recreated" studio interiors for Thomson and Dorland was a worthwhile experiment (P. 71), while the showcasing of both artists' work on opposite walls of the main exhibition space was a visually important piece of the exhibition as a whole. No juxtaposition of paintings could have been more expressive of the huge distance in time, or more suggestive of the frenetic artistry that defines Dorland's creative process (P. 72–73). Indeed, in Dorland's creative kitchen, nothing is static. Best known for pushing the boundaries of the artistic representation through exploration of memory and identity, Kim Dorland refuses to remain faithful to one medium. Experimentation with composition, colour palette, and surface embedded in heavy abstract impasto plays into the symbiotic nature of his work and adds specific intensity to the raw, fleeting quality of his paintings.

1   I wish to acknowledge the inestimable support of a few individuals who made the exhibition *You Are Here: Kim Dorland and the Return to Painting* possible. First and foremost, special thanks to the artist, Kim Dorland, and his wife, Lori, who readily embraced the vision for this exhibition: to create a dialogue with the historical collection at the McMichael. From the McMichael Canadian Art Collection, I am grateful to Dr. Victoria Dickenson, CEO, and the Board of Trustees, who lent their support, as well as to Anna Stanisz, associate director of creative learning and programs, who helped facilitate the artist-in-residence program, and to everyone at the curatorial and collections department. From the RBC, heartfelt thanks to curator Robin Anthony, without whom this publication would not have been possible, and also to Jamie Angell, the artist's dealer from Angell Gallery, for his never-ending enthusiasm and support of young artistic talents. Special thanks to all lenders who parted with their cherished works for a long period.

2   For further discussions on the origins and history of landscape painting, see Nils Büttner, *Landscape Painting: A History* (New York: Abbeville, 2006).

3   See Peter Mullen, *The Group of Seven* (Toronto: McClelland & Stewart, 1970). Kim Dorland's personal used copy (from his high-school days) was included in the exhibition as a testimony to his initial journey into the magical world of painting.

4   Author interview with Kim Dorland, September 2013.

5   Tom Thomson, letter to Dr. James MacCallum, October 6, 1914, from Canoe Lake Station. MacCallum Papers, National Gallery of Canada Archives.

6   Karen Wilkin, *David Milne: 1882–1953: Bright Garden* (Toronto: Mira Godard Gallery, 1986).

7   Thomson and the Group of Seven were credited with introducing the small wooden panel sketches as complete works of art at the turn of the twentieth century. Before them, Canada's best-known artist abroad, James W. Morrice, became very popular with his small sketches known as *pochades*.

8   Author interview with Kim Dorland, September 2013.

9   While working on the large triptych *French River* (P. 68), Kim used social media to document his daily progress and share insights from his studio work with the public.

▾ *You Are Here,* Thomson room (detail of Dorland wall),
McMichael Canadian Art Collection, Kleinburg, Ontario, 2013

▴ *You Are Here,* Dorland studio room, McMichael Canadian Art
Collection, Kleinburg, Ontario, 2013

You Are Here, Thomson room, McMichael
Canadian Art Collection, Kleinburg, Ontario, 2013

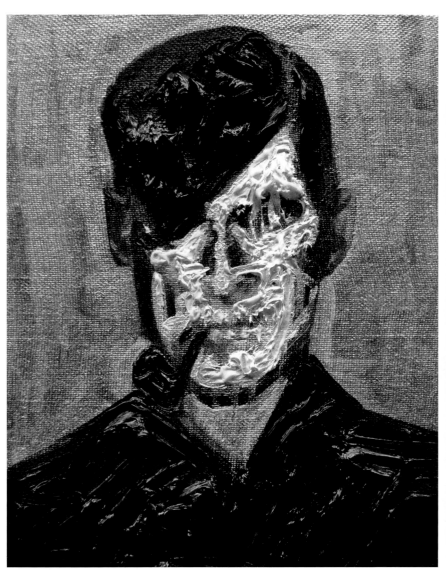

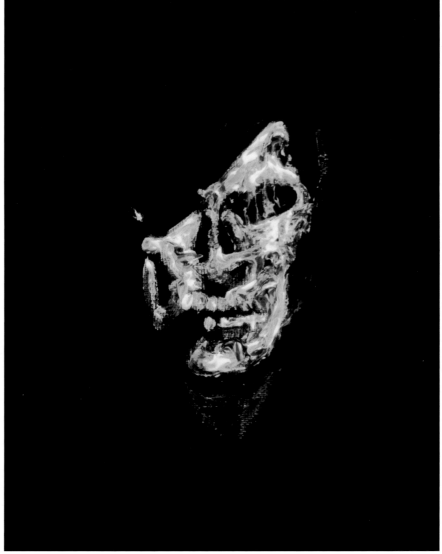

Tom Thomson (lights on) 2010
oil and acrylic on linen, 20 × 16 in.

Tom Thomson (lights off) 2010
oil and acrylic on linen, 20 × 16 in.

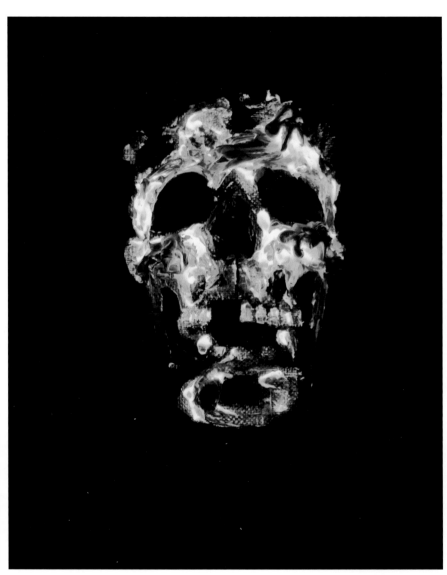

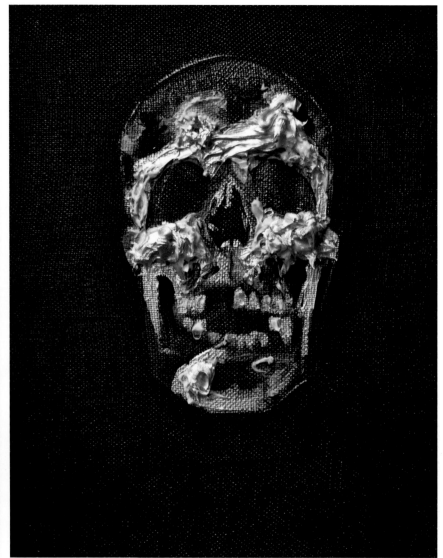

Tom Thomson's Skull **(lights off)** 2010
acrylic on linen, 20 × 16 in.

Tom Thomson's Skull **(lights on)** 2010
acrylic on linen, 20 × 16 in.

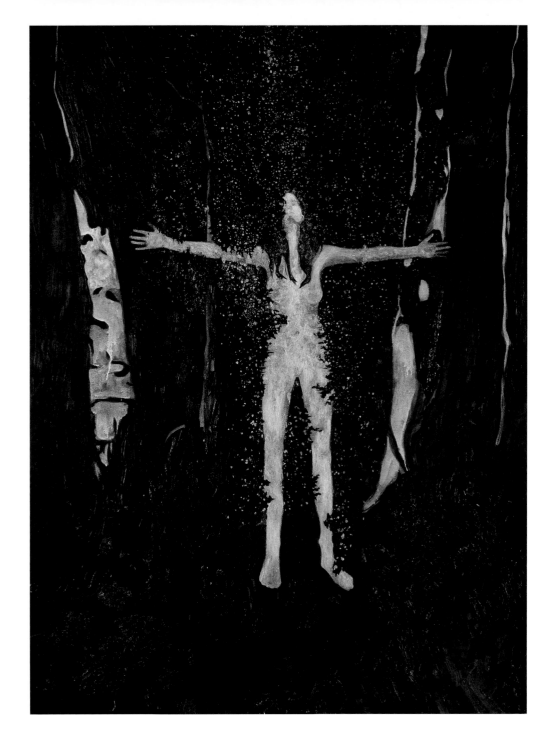

▲ *The Girl Disappears #2* 2010
oil and acrylic on canvas over wood
panel, 96 × 72 in.

▶ *Ghost* 2010
oil, acrylic, screws, and string on wood
panel, 72 × 60 in.

▲ **Shack** 2010
oil, acrylic, wood, screws, and string
on wood panel, 96 × 120 in.

▶ **Big Dead Tree** 2010
oil, acrylic, and glitter on wood
panel, 144 × 96 in.

▲ *Midnight* 2010
oil, acrylic, and gems on linen, 42 × 72 in.

▶ *Night* 2010
oil, acrylic, and glitter on wood
panel, 120 × 96 in.

▲ *Treehouse* 2010
oil, acrylic, wood, nails, and glitter
on wood panel, 96 × 72 in.

▶ *The Morning After* 2011
oil on canvas, 72 × 72 in.

▲ *Untitled (Apparition)* 2011
oil on canvas, 72 × 72 in.

▶ *Untitled (Red Sky)* 2011
oil on canvas over wood panel, 72 × 96 in.

▲ *Untitled (Thick Light)* 2011
oil on canvas over wood panel, 96 × 72 in.

▶ *Clearing* 2011
oil on wood panel, 96 × 120 in.

Shoreline, Waskesiu Lake 2011
oil on canvas over wood panel, 96 × 72 in.

Shoreline, Waskesiu Lake #2 2011
oil on canvas over wood panel, 60 × 48 in.

Shoreline, Waskesiu Lake #3 2011
oil and screws on linen over wood panel, 40 × 30 in.

▾ *Shoreline, Waskesiu Lake #4* 2011
oil on linen over wood panel, 40 × 30 in.

▴ *Shoreline, Waskesiu Lake #5* 2011
oil on linen over wood panel, 40 × 30 in.

▲ *Shoreline, Waskesiu Lake #6* 2011
oil on linen over wood panel, 40 × 30 in.

◀ *Shoreline, Waskesiu Lake #7* 2011
oil on canvas over wood panel, 48 × 36 in.

Shoreline, Waskesiu Lake #8 2011
oil and gold leaf on canvas over wood panel, 48 × 36 in.

Shoreline, Waskesiu Lake #9 2011
oil on linen over wood panel, 40 × 30 in.

Shoreline, Waskesiu Lake #10 2011
oil and screws on linen over wood panel, 40 × 30 in.

▲ *Shoreline* 2012
oil and acrylic on jute over wood
panel, 60 × 48 in.

▶ *Picnic Table* 2012
oil and wood on wood panel, 72 × 96 in.

▲ *Him #4* 2012
oil on jute over wood panel, 20 × 16 in.

▶ *Grown-ups* 2012
oil on linen, 60 × 48 in.

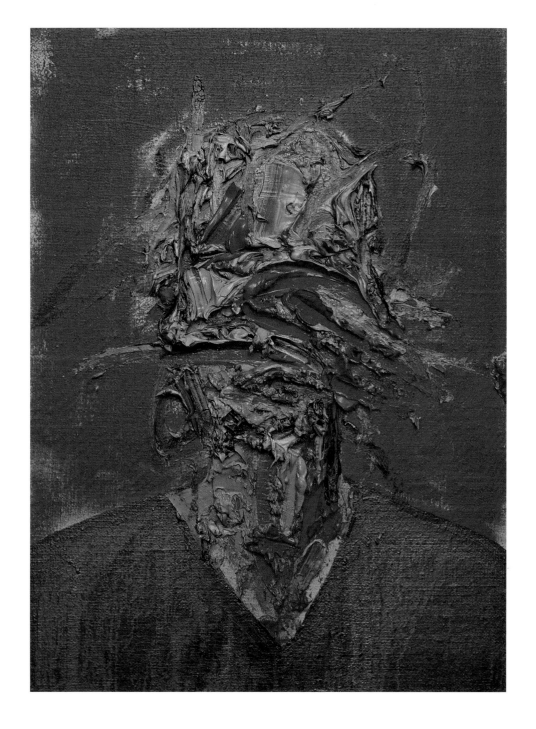

Self Portrait at 38 2012
oil on jute over wood panel, 30 × 24 in.

Magnolia 2012
oil on jute over wood panel, 48 × 36 in.

SEDUCTIONS AND AGITATIONS: AN INTERVIEW WITH KIM DORLAND

ROBERT ENRIGHT

FOR SEVERAL YEARS now, art critic Robert Enright and Kim Dorland have engaged in an ongoing dialogue about Dorland's work, and art in general. This interview is an edited collage of four conversations. The first took place in Winnipeg in 2009, the second by phone to Toronto in 2011. The third, in Toronto, was conducted in March 2013, shortly after Dorland's exhibit at the McMichael Canadian Art Collection. This discussion became the basis for an interview published in *Border Crossings* (vol. 33, no. 1, issue no. 129). The final interview was recorded at the Drake Hotel in Toronto in April 2014.

In choosing paintings for this book, you've had a chance to go back through your earlier work. What have you learned?

> What struck me was my fearlessness. I didn't expect anything at that point, so there was a youthful energy. Now that I've been painting for a long time, I'm better at it, and earnestness has been replaced with sophistication. There was also an interesting clumsiness to the work. On the other side, things haven't changed at all. The colour sense is still there and the material is definitely there, though what I call thick is definitely a lot different now. In a weird way, the work I have been doing since the McMichael exhibition is actually more like my old painting.

Alley (P.102)**, an early work, is like a scatter of pick-up sticks that reads less as landscape depiction than as a kind of abstraction. The same thing happens in the bluster of paint on the left-hand side of *The Tree on the Corner* (P.104). Were you aware at the time that you were mixing abstraction with a version of realism?**

> That was exactly what I was trying to do. My master's thesis was about combining representation and abstraction at the same time. I was trying to crumple up a piece of representation and pull it apart. I was also thinking a lot about cubism. The two things I was dealing with were abstraction and overt play.

Alley 2006
oil and acrylic on canvas over wood panel, 60 × 48 in.

In the *Fist Fight* paintings (P.106 + 107) **you literally render the act of fist fighting as a violent application of paint.**

That whole series was a way to match my paint-handling with my narrative. It was an excuse to make really violent images violently.

Was that work autobiographical? Was it about "beer and pussy," to quote a piece of graffiti from the painting?

The graffiti in *Beer and Pussy* (P. 108) perfectly defined the space I was finding myself in, and the lone figure that appears represented my relationship to that social environment. The explicit interference of the pornography in *Centrefold* (P. 109) does the same thing. It defines the space and repels me from it. It's not a representation of something I was into.

I would say that my life lives beside me. What I mean is that my paintings and the narratives they describe have evolved parallel to my evolving life. I looked back with nostalgia at the teenage stuff on the edges of suburbia; then when my life changed, I went "into the woods," literally and psychologically, until I emerged into the light of a new set of surroundings, which was the domestic life of being a father. In my work before 2005, I was stuck on what to paint and I wore a bunch of different hats, trying out different trajectories as a way of figuring out what to do. But once I was ready to look at my own life, including the nostalgic stuff, then it was "go time."

You have made a lot of zombie paintings—a number literally have "zombie" in their titles. I know some of them muse on what it's like to be a father. But I'm interested in the range of responses that you generate out of your own psyche in doing those paintings with isolated, weird figures wandering through nocturnal spaces.

I have always been a melancholy person, and it is something I battle. But those zombie paintings were a response to looking around me and noticing people. There is this new Damon Albarn album in which the title song talks about our being "everyday robots on our phones." So there is this distance, and even though we live in a very congested way, we are still separated and alone. I'm not trying to make a comment on technology, but I see a pervasive sense of sadness around me. So beyond the fact that I am a huge *Walking Dead* fan, I thought the zombies were a way to make a comment about contemporary life.

The Tree on the Corner 2007
oil, acrylic, and spray paint on canvas, 72 × 60 in.

▲ *Fist Fight #12* 2006
oil and acrylic on canvas, 78 × 62 in.

▶ *Fist Fight #6* 2006
oil and acrylic on canvas, 70 × 58 in.

▲ *Beer and Pussy* 2006
oil, acrylic, and spray paint on canvas
over wood panel, 72 × 96 in.

▶ *Centrefold* 2008
oil and acrylic on canvas, 72 × 96 in.

◄ Dufferin Street studio, Toronto, 2013

▲ Dufferin Street studio, Toronto, 2013

◄ Dufferin Street studio, Toronto, 2013

► Sterling Road studio, Toronto, 2010

Wading In (P. 113) **has an almost uncanny sense of gesture. It is a picture that precisely articulates the way the body exists in space. The same thing happens with Lori and your children in a painting at Waskesiu Lake (*Last Trip,* (P. 114)).**

I'm working from photographs, so I always have that reference, and I'm a bit of a perfectionist. Here's the thing: if I have a photograph, what I'll do is trace the photograph on a piece of vellum and paint it so that I can see what that looks like. Then I'll draw it again. Usually what I'm attracted to in a figurative pose is that perfect moment. In *Wading In*, there is something about the weight of my shoulders and the way my arm is hanging that tells you I am about thirty-five years old. *Dripping Dream* (P. 61) is another example; I really wanted to hit that pose, so I practised it. If I want the pose to be deadpan perfect, I'll project it. My method is a mishmash. *Dripping Dream* was like that; I projected the figure to get that back perfect, next I drew it, followed by a small painting. You edit until it is perfect, and then you totally invent the background.

You do a kind of landscape painting, like *Super! Natural!* (P. 115), where you risk letting innocence run wild, where animals that would normally devour one another happily co-exist in the same environment.

Those paintings are meant to be funny and to poke fun at Canadiana. Sometimes you have to think about your audience. *Super! Natural!* was done for an American audience in New York. I liked the idea of toying with America's perception of what it is to be a Canadian. I'm still asked if I ride a snowmobile to my studio.

You have some pretty unconventional animals in your painting. You push nature in directions that are not natural.

I guess that has always been caused by my healthy fear of nature. I'm not an outdoorsman, and even as I get older and more confident, I'm still an observer of nature and not a participant. That was my way of making those animals as distant and otherworldly as I could possibly make them.

Wading In 2012
oil on jute over wood panel, 72 × 60 in.

Last Trip 2013
oil and acrylic on wood panel, 9 × 12 in.

Super! Natural! 2009
oil and acrylic on wood panel, 96 × 144 in.

Sometimes they're frightening, and at others they are almost exquisite.

It's total reverence. I am in awe of nature but I'm also scared to death of it.

You have always said that one of the things you want to do is paint light. Is the attempt to capture the range, gradations, and structure of light an ongoing pursuit?

Totally. I tend to work in bodies of work. My last show in New York included a painting called *The End* (P. 117) about light bleeding through. The nature that I paint is generally very specific, but that nature was a little more orchestrated, as if it were at the end of a movie. I don't work the way I used to. I don't go into the studio and do a painting and leave. Right now, I have six or seven paintings that are maybe 10 percent done. I'm happy moving through them and seeing how things work out. I have the time to consider things and to build the paintings quite slowly, so there are fewer paintings that don't work now than there were in the past. The difference between me then and now is that, in the past, if I had a painting that was failing, I would go with it until the very end. *March Break* (P. 118), the painting of Seymour diving, is a good example; halfway through I was confused about what to do, so rather than just trying something and have it go down, I took another piece of paper that was exactly the same size and built it to that same point. I tried things out on the piece of paper and then I moved over to the painting.

It seems that what you choose to paint often comes out of your ruminating or looking at other painters. So in *For Matisse* (P. 119), you are clearly looking at his work. Painting for you is generative in that way?

Influence is not something I'm afraid of. But I loved the Peter Doig show in Montreal so much that I had to deal with it in a different way. I expected to love the show, but I didn't know how much of a kick in the teeth it would be. It's absolutely magnificent, and I had to take that back to my studio and to work through it. I had to be really uncomfortable for a while to let that influence through, let it move past me, and then claim it for my own.

The End 2013
oil on linen, 72 × 96 in.

▲ *March Break* 2014
oil, acrylic, and spray paint on linen
over wood panel, 60 × 48 in.

▶ *For Matisse* 2008
oil on wood panel, 96 × 96 in.

March Break has a Doig-like quality to it.

It does, and when I was working on the painting it really had a Doig-like quality, and rather than hide from it, which is what you want to do, I said, "Fuck it, I'm going to do my painting and I'm going to work through my influence here." I came through it. If I were to see him again, I'd thank him for his show. There are definitely matters of poise and the way his paintings are structured that I want to take and make my own. I don't want to borrow; I want to steal. He is magic; he has that touch. There's a sense of perfection to his work.

I want to step back and ask, when did you first get involved with landscape painting?

We would spend a month or two every year in my wife's family cabin in northern Saskatchewan. I don't go deep into the landscape, or hunt, or anything like that. But every time I was there, I would take hundreds of photographs and bring back the experience with me. There's a painting from 2007 of the northern lights (_Northern Lights,_ (P. 55)) that is a direct experience in nature. I would say that 90 percent of the landscapes I have painted have some kind of interruption or interference. For me it was always about shining a light on that. The McMichael show was an anomaly because it was about interacting with the permanent collection, which I wanted to do in a way that paid respect to the artists.

How did it work?

There were two ways the artist-in-residence thing could have gone; I could have been on the grounds physically doing work, but I wasn't so interested in that, mostly because I need access to spray paint and my airbrush machine. Also, the scale of my work and the amount of material I use made it impossible. So it turned into an exploration of the collection. There were some specific paintings that I wanted to respond to by Thomson and J.E.H. MacDonald, as well as a very weird Frank Johnston. My biggest fear was that it could become confrontational. I didn't want to go toe to toe with Thomson, mostly because of my utmost respect for him as a painter. I also didn't want to set myself up as this cocky person.

What is it about Thomson that you respond to in such a passionate way?

I am very attracted to his myth. He wasn't the most talented or naturally gifted member of the Group. I think Lawren Harris was more elegantly talented, but Thomson was self-taught and he was rough. He got better and better and better through the work, which is how I proceed. He was also a brilliant colourist, and the way he used material was perfect.

You come at his myth in two ways; in *Seconds Before* (P. 65), you have him standing in his canoe urinating before he falls and drowns.

It's a little joke. I was leading the Emma Lake Artists' Workshop in Saskatchewan when I did the painting, so I was steeped in that narrative. I was able to pick perspectives on his death and play with them. It was also the first time that I had painted *en plein air*.

In the McMichael exhibition, you included a painting of what was purported to be his skull set against a bed of autumnal leaves (*October 5, 1956* (yellow version), (P. 123)).

That painting is based on the three or four ghouls who dug up his body in 1956. That was the skull they pulled up. It is such a fascinating image of debauchery: digging up a dead body and then taking pictures. There was something so garish about what they did that I had to paint it.

You paint it in such a way that there is an indentation on the surface. The hole in the skull suggests that foul play was involved in his death, so you engage another variation on the myth.

I highlighted the hole and made it the most obvious part. But I was also interested in the formal thing of altering the canvas. It was nice to be able to physically carve the hole. The leaves in the background were in the photograph. I actually made the pilgrimage up there in the fall, and those are true colours. The McMichael show definitely highlighted my influences, but the other point of the exhibition was to show that I'm not carrying the torch of the Group of Seven. I'm not Tom Junior. When I signed on, that was a concern. Sometimes your decisions can pigeonhole you, so I wanted to be clear that I have my influences, but

I have my own thing too. One of those things was to take pristine nature and find ways to subvert it by bringing in that sinister edge. I think it also reflects my experience of nature, especially deep nature, where a primal fear occurs. I show that through the phantoms and the Sasquatches and the graffiti.

In a previous conversation you told me that the figure of the Sasquatch is a self-portrait. Is he an aspect of you in nature?

I think so. Or the Sasquatch is equally a portrait of someone like Tom Thomson. It represents something mythic that can't be pinned down. There is something tragically interesting about that type of figure. They're scary, but they're sad and alone.

Yours is essentially a romantic view of nature. Even the painting of the zombie family (*Zombies #3 (Family)* (P.125)) is not frightening. You don't quite know what they're doing in the landscape at midnight, but they're not going to cause anyone any trouble. What is also interesting is that the painting clearly takes as its point of departure MacDonald's *In November* (P.124) from 1917.

I adore my family, and that painting is about being a family man. But it's also about how hard it is to be a family person. It's not only the father and mother who feel that; the kids feel it too. So it dealt with the idea of that sometime drudgery. I also liked creating a narrative that made no sense: Why are they walking into the woods so late at night?

The noticeable formal quality is the buildup of thick paint in the sky. The material tribute to the MacDonald source painting is there.

I responded to the way he made light in that sky. The time of day and this time of year is perfect for me because everything becomes paintable, so that was my response to the melancholy nature of that painting. My idea was to take the beautiful sky and also the mid-ground trees, the middle distance, and change the colour. It is a pretty simple composition, so it gives me licence to do something crazy with the clouds.

October 5, 1956 (yellow version) 2011
oil and acrylic on linen over canvas, 16 × 20 in.

▲ J.E.H. MacDonald, *In November* 1917
  oil on paperboard, 21 × 26 in.

▶ *Zombies #3 (Family)* 2013
  oil on jute over wood panel, 72 × 92 in.

That notion of where you are as the maker, and where we are as viewers in your work, is interesting. In the larger overall frame of the paintings, the figures are often too small; the landscape rising above them is disproportionate to their size, and because of the nature of the marks, things become almost abstract. Is that a deliberate playing around with scale and spatial relationships?

I'll use any way to make my figures and the viewer uncomfortable. I'm not interested in a compositionally correct painting. *Untitled (Red Smoker)* (P. 128) has everything wrong about it; the linen is too thick, the figure is wonky and totally minor inside the big landscape. For me, all those components build to something that is psychologically more intense and more interesting.

Why do you want to disrupt the viewer's experience?

Even when I was doing representation with a bit of abstraction added, my idea was always simple: make it evident that it is a painting and make the painting both seduce and repulse the viewer at the same time. Comfort for me is almost impossible. I'm not a comfortable person, and ultimately the paintings are all about me. I love what I do, I love the act of making things, but it's not a comfortable relationship. Painting is an agitation.

You used paint in very different ways throughout the McMichael exhibition. I'm thinking of *Tom Thomson* (P.129), the portrait you made in 2009, in which he is wearing his trademark hat. The work has an especially thick application of paint. How do you determine how much paint you have to layer on?

The painting always tells me. The portraits tend to work that way because they require a lot of time, and I'm trying to make the painting the sitter in a way. So it isn't just what they look like; it's what they seem like, what they feel like. Hopefully, I capture something of Lori and my kids when I paint them. But when it comes to other paintings that were in the show, there was no ingredients list; I just felt the space should be more solid, and for me, solid is a lot of paint. It's a very intuitive process. I still need to tack the paint onto the surface. In the Tom Thomson portrait, the paint is screwed in. I work the portraits in layers. I let it dry for six months on its back, put in some screws, and

Dufferin Street studio, Toronto, 2013

126

start building again. Frank Auerbach, Leon Kossoff, and Lucian Freud were big influences. They're heavy painters. *You Are Here* was definitely about Thomson and the Group, but I'm an omnivore when it comes to my paintings and there are countless more influences. I don't hide from them.

I want to talk about the painting in the McMichael exhibition where you most literally paid attention to the source, *Woodland Waterfall (after Tom Thomson)* (P. 63).

I did that on purpose. I wanted to do one complete appropriation, and I thought it was a really good choice. First of all, the sketch is a typically great Thomson, whereas the big painting is problematic and odd. The space doesn't allow you a lot of room to move around. In a way, it looks like a hipster did that painting with some kind of cool detachment. When I did my version, I had both images on my large piece of cardboard in the studio room. I had to figure it out, bring it really close to Thomson, and then completely dismantle it and redo it as my painting.

The water becomes a shape more than the representation of a natural element.

Yes. Even though it's representational, it is the most abstract painting I have ever done. I am happy with the way the weird spray-paint blobs came out. It really challenged me because it was predominantly colours I never use. I don't even think I own earth tones, so it was fun to figure out different ways to mix them. Parts of that painting could go in a future direction, and not necessarily in a pure landscape way. It has an oddness that I like. Sometimes you recognize a touch in your own painting and you would like to see where it ends up.

Some of the smaller portraits of Lori are very Munch-like. He spooks your landscapes on occasion.

I'm attracted to the charge of Munch's paintings. They have so much emotion, and there is something special about his ability to convey his own sense of alienation and dread. He was such an elegant colourist and had such a refined but rough line. He was full of contradictions, which usually makes for good work.

▲ *Untitled (Red Smoker)* 2013
oil and acrylic on jute over wood panel, 11 × 14 in.

▶ *Tom Thomson* 2009
oil and acrylic on wood panel, 20 × 16 in.

So, do your contradictions emerge naturally, or do you have to cultivate them?

The contradictions are very natural. If you start to think too much, it can kill the art. I do what interests me. A better way to answer your question is that I'm not so deliberate in my choices.

How does influence work? Is it retinal memory?

For me, it's something that gets under your skin and you have to find a way to work with it. You can mask it and hide it and try to run from your influences, or you can face them. As I've said, I have a lot of influences. Often I'm more attracted to the weirdoes. I'm a huge Daniel Richter fan, but I'm also a Charles Burchfield fan. There is so much great painting out there, and I want to find a way to speak to it. Right now I am really interested in Diebenkorn's figurative works and in Manet and Matisse. I find it harder to look at the art of my time. I can see where my work is going and it is definitely in a different direction from the one I was on, which is exciting. I'm only in the vague stage, but I'm definitely interested in a zeitgeist of disconnection that seems pervasive. I need to find a way to figure that out and to make paintings out of it.

You often employ an intense line, in the *Dripping Dream* paintings, for example. When I look at those, I think of Milne. You take his chair from *Blue Interior* (1913) and set it in the landscape as part of your *en plein air* studio.

Milne is one of the most sophisticated painters I've ever seen, and I think he is an amazing artist. But the easels in the woods are from photos I took at Emma Lake. The crazy thing is that you would go walking in the woods and you'd find an easel. Somebody may have been too lazy to bring it back or forgot that they had left it there. But it created this eerie, weird feeling.

I thought the easel without a painter was another reference to Thomson as the absent painter. Then in *You Are Here* (P. 42), the title piece of the McMichael exhibition, you're standing at that same easel. So, mixed together are present and absent painters.

It is up to the viewer to decide which painter is absent, and that forced choice generates a nice psychological tension. I was actually freaked out working *en plein air* because it is overwhelmingly hard. There is so much going on, you have to pick points, you have to edit on the spot, and you generally have just a teeny little panel because you want it to be portable. So with *Dripping Dream* and *You Are Here*, I had to psychologically place myself inside that situation through my own paintings.

Your paintings engage an interesting dialogue with representation. In some of the landscapes, dark trees painted in very black paint can be read quite realistically. It's almost *trompe l'oeil*. Were you deliberately evoking a certain kind of realism?

There are two things going on. When I make oil paint look like something it's not, when I'm carving a relief or something, I want it to represent physicality. So the trees in the background of *Dripping Dream* have that lusciousness. But there is also a play on perspective, so the closest trees are the flattest, and the ones farthest away are the thickest. It's another way to take the viewer's expectations and turn them on their head. Grabbing the viewer and holding them is what painting does best, and for that to happen, everything has to be working. Because I'm not interested in beauty for beauty's sake. There have to be other things going on.

The difference between *Woods #2* (P. 133) and *Woods #4* (P. 132) is that the former is almost realistic, while the latter goes in the opposite direction. Do those two paintings of what is essentially the same subject frame the breadth of your approach to landscape painting?

Yes. *Woods #2* is a real place that I took a photo of (I still have the photo in my studio), and it is a space I saw every day when I was walking my dog. *Woods #4* is an invention and is more psychological. I can play inside that kind of psychological space and create the tone, whereas in *Woods #2* the tone is there and I'm trying to capture it.

▲ *Woods #4* 2008
oil, acrylic, spray paint, and ink on
wood panel, 96 × 216 in.

▶ *Woods #2* 2008
oil, acrylic, and spray paint on canvas
over wood panel, 60 × 72 in.

You transferred an entire wall from your studio to the McMichael exhibition. It included a large number of small paintings, sketches, newspaper clippings, and two iPads encased in the wall itself (P. 71, 135)**. Looking at the iPad was intriguing—it showed the flaring you got while videotaping out the car window during a trip you took with your family. That flaring becomes a structure of light in the final paintings.**

That was the initial idea, and all those paintings came from that video. I was using a crappy iPhone lens—I think it was an iPhone 3—and so it kept flooding and turned into this amazing, flashing thing. It was like the sun was following me. It's a weird video, and I wouldn't say it's art, but it was worth showing as a piece that influenced other pieces.

As the paintings are being made, so much paint is going down, with so many variations on thickness, texture, and gesture. When you're in the moment, how much are you thinking about what you're doing?

I would say it is fifty-fifty. What happens with my painting is that I get obsessed with an idea, and then a suite of paintings will revolve around that idea. I keep trying to find different ways to express it, so in the case of light, there was thick light/thin light and what was in between. In the act, I'm not thinking so much, but afterward I'll step back and see what I've done. Then I might go back in and make different decisions. Most often I do the painting and that's it, but there are a number of works, like *Untitled (Heavy Beams)* (P. 67), which I had done up to a certain point and couldn't figure out how to finish. I worked on it for a few months and eventually figured out how to resolve the taped-up part. Sometimes that happens. I still have paintings in storage that I want to finish.

One of the things that the studio wall indicated was that you do a lot of studies. Are they preparatory, or do you use them to figure something out in the process of working on a painting?

Sometimes they come after because I want to see what the directness of pencil, crayon, or watercolour will offer. There are also occasions where it is enjoyable to take a huge idea and make it small. That wall will keep me busy for years to come.

You Are Here, Dorland studio room, McMichael Canadian Art Collection, Kleinburg, Ontario, 2013

When you work on a small scale, how do you develop a rhythm?

I do it by having many pieces on the go at the same time. Generally, I wouldn't put up a small panel and work on it; I would put up ten, along with all my source images and drawings and watercolours. I'll go over to one part and make a certain kind of mark, and then I'll make a very different kind of mark on another. It's basically like working on one big painting because there are so many different elements, and every little painting needs a different piece of that approach.

Do you still work directly with paint squeezed out of the tube?

I work less from the tube than you might think. Mostly it's brushes and knives. I realized I was spending thousands of dollars a year on brushes because I was too lazy to clean them, so I forced myself to buy very expensive brushes, which I now clean.

Green Tree, Blue Tree #2 (P. 49) **is viscerally powerful. It's more about painting than it is a depiction of a landscape.**

Yes, it's edging toward non-representation. I used a one-and-a-half-inch palette knife so that I could pile the paint up and drag it, and then go over it again and again and again until I got the smoosh. It's faster than you'd think. They look slow and sluggish, but that painting probably took only a day or two. The trees were the final decisions, and they would have taken only a couple of hours to make. I did everything else, and then thought I have to do something interesting with the palette knife to change the reading of this painting.

In a similar way, many of your portraits of Lori are more about painting than portraiture.

Everybody knows how much I love Lori, but I'm also fascinated with her, so I'm searching something out in those paintings. They can be pretty ghastly, tough paintings. I did a whole Lori portrait show in New York and I was accused of flaying her to pieces. I can see why that reading is there, but it has nothing to do with what I'm thinking. For me, they're loving portraits.

You've done portraits, landscapes, nudes. Have you systematically worked through the categories of painting?

I do what interests me. I like to ask a lot of my audience: *You're expecting this, but how about this?* It's also a way of keeping it exciting for me. Who wants to do the same painting over and over again? I'm restless, and so I don't want to work with the imagery from the McMichael show for a while. It was a great experience, but it's time

Her, exhibition view, Parisian Laundry, Montreal 2009

to move on to some new material. I'm definitely looking more at my own life now. In the Alberta work, I was looking back at my life to figure out where that life was going. At this point, I don't need to look very far to find intense relationships. I have my children and my wife and that is enough.

You had done nudes before, in 2008, in *For Matisse* (P.119) and *Coy Girl* (P.138), but the new work indicates a domestic eroticism. What provoked these recent paintings?

I definitely wanted to do something personally intimate after the McMichael show. I think the difference between the new work of Lori and *Coy Girl* and *For Matisse* is that those paintings were materially bombastic; the subject was almost an excuse to flex paint. Whereas the recent paintings are actually intimate portraits in which I'm trying to display my affection and love for this other person. But the moves I make are always kind of a whim. I want to see what something looks like, but instead of doing one or two versions, I'll do twenty. I'll take twenty or thirty Polaroids of Lori and go from there. She is an all-purpose inspiration for me. Even in my early works from 2006 she was always in the bush party. If you look closely, you'll see that Lori is in there five or six times. I know her so well that I could draw her right now: back, front, side, sitting, standing. I could draw her from my head because we are always in the same space. She's in my studio all day. As you get older your world gets smaller, especially with kids.

How do you decide what medium to use?

It would be lovely to do everything in acrylic because you don't have drying issues, but I love oil paint. Now that I'm getting older, I've got a catalogue in my head. I know so many different brands and how they react to different mediums. It's a very, very intelligent medium, and it takes a long time to get to know it well, and I'm just getting there. It's impossible to set that much knowledge aside. I've been painting with oil for twenty-two years, and until you physically experience it, it's knowledge that is not available to you.

You have talked in the past about colour as an almost magical process. Your palette is an unusual one.

It is an eccentric palette. There are some deliberate choices, so I will say this needs to be muted, or this needs to be super keyed, but the actual colour choices seem to come from an unnatural mixing of things. I have a pretty good idea of how to get to certain places with colour.

You refer to the disruptions in your work, which can be very funny. Do you think the paintings are funny?

Sometimes they are ridiculous. I feel I have a pretty dark sense of humour. Socially, humour is a powerful tool in helping you cope with terrible things. There are little moments in the painting, like Tom Thomson peeing off the canoe, or the Sasquatch standing at the edge of the water, that are meant to be funny. There is something about that little Sasquatch that I really connect with. But it is an odd choice. Beyond painting, one of my great loves is stand-up comedy. I'm a huge fan of Louis C.K. and Sarah Silverman. I think the way they work is similar to painting: they create something out of nothing by observing what is going on around them and admitting their own failures. Louis C.K. is a genius; look at the way he makes you uncomfortable so that you'll question things. And Silverman is beautiful and charming. She's like Ross Bleckner, very elegant.

Early in our conversation you mentioned seduction. Is seduction part of the strategy?

Yes, because oil paint is inherently beautiful, and paintings have to operate with some element of beauty. I don't want to go all the way because then you end up with something that is inert.

You now accept unmediated beauty, but there was a period when you'd make something beautiful and then mess with it. You have obviously abandoned the necessity of self-sabotage.

Yes. I think self-sabotage is interesting, but I don't think it needs to be the motivation to make art. Cynicism always gets old, but beauty never does.

Coy Girl 2008
oil on wood panel, 96 × 96 in.

▼ *New Material,* exhibition view, Mike Weiss
Gallery, New York, 2010

▲ *About a Girl,* exhibition view, Angell Gallery,
Toronto, 2007

◄ *Her*, exhibition view, Parisian Laundry, Montreal 2009

► *Nocturne,* exhibition view, Angell Gallery, Toronto, 2011

Feb. 2, 2011 2013
oil and acrylic on wood panel, 9 × 12 in.

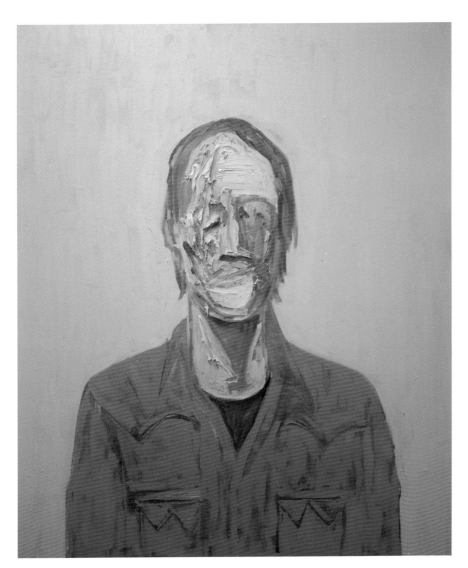

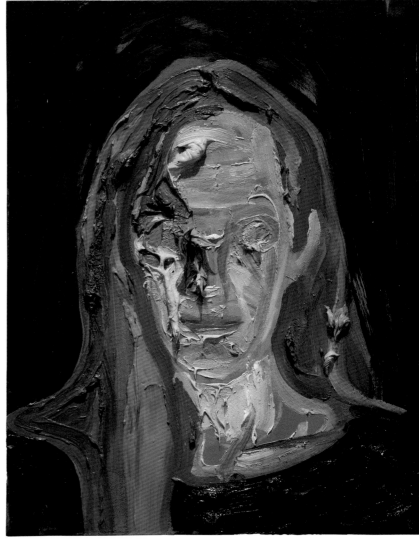

▲ *Self* 2013
oil and acrylic over wood panel, 72 × 60 in.

◀ *Untitled (Sevres Green Lori)* 2013
oil and acrylic on wood panel, 10 × 8 in.

T. Dorland 2013
oil and acrylic on wood panel, 9 × 12 in.

▲ *Zombies (Parents)* 2013
oil on canvas over wood panel, 72 × 60 in.

▶ *Zombies* 2013
oil and acrylic on jute over wood panel, 72 × 96 in.

▲ *Ghost Moose* 2013
oil and acrylic on canvas over wood
panel, 60 × 48 in.

▶ *Untitled (Thomson Canoe)* 2013
oil and acrylic on jute over wood panel,
48 × 60 in.

▲ *Stream* 2013
   oil and acrylic on wood panel, 11 × 14 in.

▶ *Northern Lights* 2013
   oil and acrylic on wood panel, 11 × 14 in.

▲ *Sasquatch/Shoreline* 2013
oil and acrylic on linen over wood panel,
11 × 14 in.

▶ *The Place* 2013
oil and acrylic on linen over wood panel,
10 × 8 in.

▲ *Death by Landscape (for M.A.),*
or *The Girl Disappears #4* 2013
oil and acrylic on canvas over wood
panel, 120 × 84 in.

▶ *Little Joe Lake* 2013
oil and acrylic on jute over wood
panel, 11 × 14 in.

Margaret Lane 2014
oil, acrylic, and screws on canvas over
wood panel, 48 × 60 in.

Stanley Park 2014
oil, acrylic, and screws on canvas over
wood panel, 60 × 48 in.

Untitled (Lori, door frame) 2014
oil and acrylic on canvas over wood panel,
40 × 30 in.

▲ **Untitled (Lori, Reclining, Green)** 2014
  oil and acrylic on linen over wood panel,
  16 × 20 in.

▶ **Bay Blanket #2** 2014
  oil and acrylic on linen over wood panel,
  40 × 30 in.

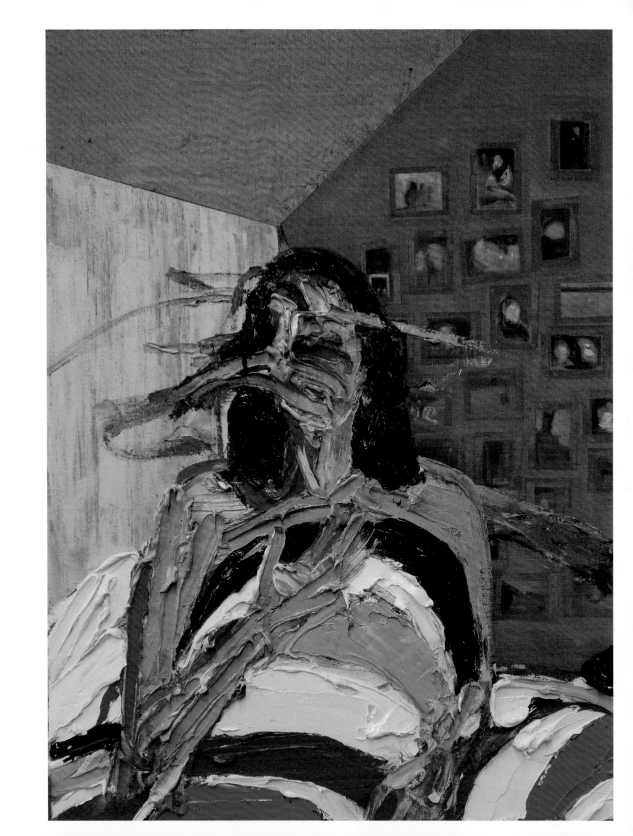

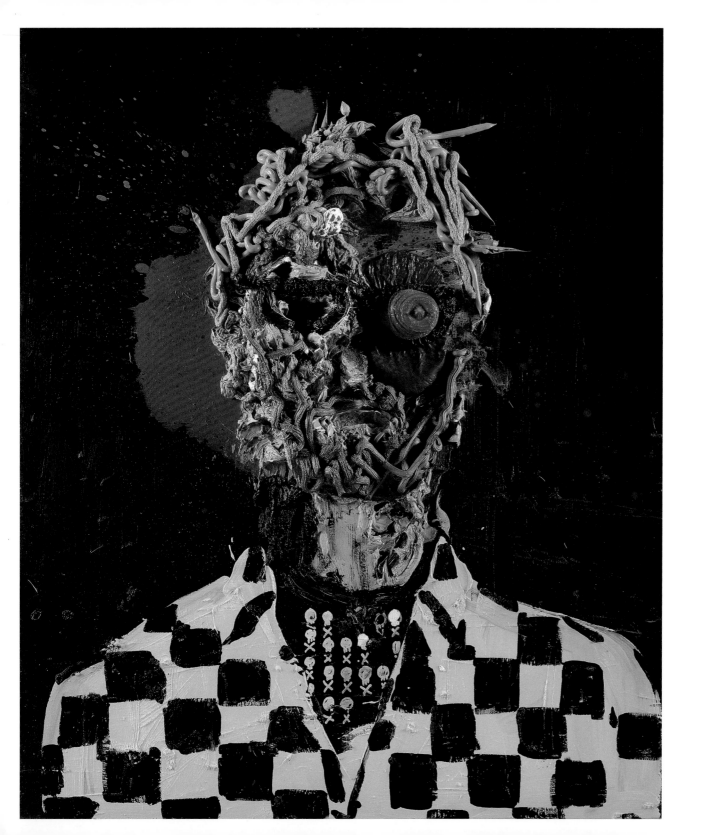

ABOUT
THE ARTIST

KIM DORLAND pushes the boundaries of painted representation through an exploration of memory, material, nostalgia, identity, and place. Drawing heavily from the Canadian landscape and his voracious appetite for the history and language of painting, the loose yet identifiable scenes are interjected with areas of heavy abstract impasto, adding to the raw, fleeting quality of his canvases.

Born in 1974 in Wainwright, Alberta, Dorland holds an MFA from York University in Toronto, and a BFA from the Emily Carr Institute of Art and Design in Vancouver. He has exhibited globally, including shows in Milan, New York, Chicago, and Los Angeles. His work is featured in the Sander Collection (Berlin); Musée des beaux-arts de Montréal; Musée d'art contemporain de Montréal; Glenbow Museum (Calgary); Museum of Contemporary Art San Diego, and numerous private collections. Dorland works in Toronto, where he lives with his wife, Lori, and their two children, Seymour and Thomson.

Self in a Checkered Shirt 2008
oil and acrylic on wood panel, 36 × 30 in.

EXHIBITIONS AND COLLECTIONS

SOLO EXHIBITIONS

2014

- *Kim Dorland: Homecoming*, Contemporary Calgary, Calgary, Alberta
- *I Hate Poetry, But I Love TV*, Angell Gallery, Toronto, Ontario
- *Kim Dorland* (solo booth), Volta NY, New York

2013

- *You Are Here: Kim Dorland and the Return to Painting*, McMichael Canadian Art Collection, Kleinburg, Ontario
- *Ghosts of You and Me*, Mike Weiss Gallery, New York

2012

- *I'm an Adult Now,* Angell Gallery, Toronto
- *Unexpected Beauty,* Galleria Bianca, Palermo, Italy

2011

- *Kim Dorland* (solo booth), Art Toronto, Angell Gallery, Toronto
- *Enter Light,* Galerie Division, Montreal
- *For Lori,* Mike Weiss Gallery, New York
- *Nocturne,* Angell Gallery, Toronto

2010

- *New Material,* Mike Weiss Gallery, New York
- *1991,* Mark Moore Gallery, Santa Monica
- *Kim Dorland* (solo booth), Mark Moore Gallery, PULSE Contemporary Art Fair, New York

2009

- *Canadian Content,* Skew Gallery, Calgary
- *Kim Dorland,* Bonelli ArteContemporanea, Mantova, Italy
- *Super! Natural!* Freight + Volume, New York
- *Kim Dorland,* Mark Moore Gallery, Santa Monica
- *Her,* Parisian Laundry, Montreal

2008

- *4 Portraits and a Landscape,* Angell Gallery, Toronto
- *North,* Freight + Volume, New York (catalogue)

2007

- *Somewhere in the Neighborhood,* Bonelli Contemporary, Los Angeles
- *About a Girl,* Angell Gallery, Toronto
- *Over the Fence,* Skew Gallery, Calgary
- Kim Dorland, Centro Culturale Cascina Grande, Rozzano, Italy (curated by Maria Chiara Valacchi)

2006

- *The Edge of Town,* Kasia Kay Art Projects, Chicago
- *Kim Dorland,* Angell Gallery, Toronto
- *Into the Woods,* Contemporaneamente, Milan (catalogue)

2005

- *Kim Dorland,* Skew Gallery, Calgary
- *doubletake,* Angell Gallery, Toronto

2004

- *Paintings of Desire,* Angell Gallery, Toronto

2003

- *Overload,* Katharine Mulherin Contemporary Art Projects, Toronto

2002

- exquisitenorth, Luft Gallery, Toronto
- Sun of the Golden West, 1080BUS Gallery, Toronto

2001

- It Looks Like Art, West Wing Gallery, Toronto

GROUP EXHIBITIONS

2014

- *I <3 Paint,* Angell Gallery, Toronto (curated by Kim Dorland)
- *Landscape,* Showcase/Megumi Ogita Gallery, Tokyo

2013

- *More Than Two (Let It Make Itself),* The Power Plant Contemporary Art Gallery, Toronto (catalogue)
- *The Painting Project,* Galerie de l'UQAM, Montreal (catalogue)
- *True North,* Harbourfront Centre, Toronto

2012

- *It Happened in the Woods,* Hans Alf Gallery, Copenhagen
- *Oppenheimer@20,* Nerman Museum of Contemporary Art, Kansas City, Kansas (catalogue)
- *60 Painters,* Humber Arts and Media Studios, Humber College, Toronto (catalogue)
- *Eileen S. Kaminsky Family Foundation New Acquisitions and Prints,* Mana Contemporary, Jersey City, New Jersey
- *The Tree: Form and Substance,* McMichael Canadian Art Collection, Kleinburg, Ontario
- *Idealizing the Imaginary: Illusion and Invention in Contemporary Painting,* Oakland University Art Gallery, Rochester, Michigan

2011

- *Oye Chica!* The Mission Projects, Chicago
- Grand opening, Eileen S. Kaminsky Family Foundation, Jersey City, New Jersey
- *Paper A-Z,* Sue Scott Gallery, New York
- *OPEN,* Mark Moore Gallery, Santa Monica

2010

- *Peinture Extreme,* Galerie Division, Montreal
- *Reflexive Self,* Mike Weiss Gallery, New York
- *Natural Renditions,* Marlborough Chelsea, New York

2009

- *Holy Destruction,* Galerie Polad-Hardouin, Paris (catalogue)
- *SUBSTANTIAL RESOURCES,* Art Gallery of Sudbury, Sudbury, Ontario
- *Home,* Westport Arts Center, Westport, Connecticut
- *Giving Face: Portraits for a New Generation,* Nicholas Robinson Gallery, New York (curated by Stephen Heighton)

2008

- *Carte Blanche Volume 2: Painting,* Museum of Contemporary Canadian Art, Toronto
- *People,* Jim Kempner Fine Art, New York

2007

- *Rear/View,* Freight + Volume, New York (curated by Eric Shiner)
- *Out Behind the Shed,* Richard A. and Rissa W. Grossman Gallery, Lafayette College, Easton, Pennsylvania
- *RBC Canadian Painting Competition Exhibition,* Ontario College of Art and Design, Toronto; Galerie d'art Louise-et-Reuben-Cohen, Université de Moncton, Moncton, New Brunswick; MacLaren Art Centre, Barrie, Ontario; Winnipeg Art Gallery, Winnipeg, Manitoba; Emily Carr Institute of Art and Design, Vancouver
- *Gary Goldstein, Jenny Dubnau, Kim Dorland and Sally Heller,* Jim Kempner Fine Art, New York
- *Oil Spill: New Paintings in Ontario,* SAW Gallery, Ottawa

- *Summer Group Show,* Bonelli Contemporary, Los Angeles
- *Notions of Wilderness,* Kasia Kay Art Projects, Chicago

2006

- *RBC Canadian Painting Competition Exhibition,* Museum of Contemporary Canadian Art, Toronto; Kitchener-Waterloo Art Gallery, Kitchener, Ontario; Musée d'art contemporain de Montréal, Montreal; Art Gallery of Calgary, Calgary; Contemporary Art Gallery, Vancouver
- *3 Painters,* Howard House, Seattle
- *The Daily Constitutional, Kim Dorland, Bruce Wilhelm,* ADA Gallery, Richmond, Virginia
- *Impression/Ism: Contemporary Impressions,* City of Brea Art Gallery, Brea, California (catalogue)

2005

- *You Don't Want to Miss That Shit: Contemporary Painters at the Gladstone Hotel,* Toronto (curated by Katharine Mulherin)
- *Blame Canada,* Harvey Levine Gallery, Los Angeles

2004

- *Best of BUS: Volume 1,* Katharine Mulherin Contemporary Art Projects, Toronto
- *Little Stabs at Happiness,* Clint Roenisch Gallery, Toronto

SELECTED PERMANENT COLLECTIONS

- ALDO Group, Montreal
- Bank of Montreal, Montreal
- The Beth Rudin DeWoody Collection
- Blanton Museum of Art at the University of Texas
- Eileen S. Kaminsky Family Foundation, New York
- The Glenbow Museum, Calgary
- Musée d'art contemporain de Montréal, Montreal,
- Musée des beaux-arts de Montréal, Montreal
- Museum of Contemporary Art San Diego, San Diego
- The Neumann Family Collection, New York
- Oppenheimer Collection, Nerman Museum of Contemporary Art, Kansas City, Kansas
- The Richard Massey Foundation, New York
- Richard Prince
- Royal Bank of Canada
- The Sander Collection, Berlin

SELECTED BIBLIOGRAPHY

2014

- Enright, Robert. "Painting's Giant Dialogue: An Interview with Kim Dorland." *Border Crossings* 33, 1 (issue 129) (March 2014).

2013

- Adams, James. "Globe Arts' Artist of the Year, Kim Dorland: Champion of the Wild." *Globe and Mail,* December 28, 2013.
- ——. "The Natural." *Globe and Mail,* October 26, 2013.
- Angel, Sara. "Like Tom Thomson on Acid." *Maclean's,* October 28, 2013.
- Featured artist, *Arc Poetry Magazine,* Summer 2013.
- Kalm, James. "Kim Dorland 'Ghosts of You and Me' at Mike Weiss Gallery, Rough Cuts." May 3, 2013. www.youtube.com/watch?v=OG_Z_PNQGDU.
- Laluyan, Oscar. "AF Best in Show & Year in Review 2013." *Arte Fuse,* December 30, 2013.
- Milroy, Sarah. "Is That the Forest Pressing In, or the Group of Seven?" *Globe and Mail,* April 26, 2013.
- Powis, Tim. "Beautiful Stuff: Kim Dorland's Love of Paint Knows No Bounds." *Canadian Art,* Spring 2013.
- "The Morning After." *Harper's,* June 2013.
- Rhodes, Richard. Reviews: "Kim Dorland." *Canadian Art,* Winter 2013.

- Whyte, Murray. "Changing the Landscape." *Toronto Star,* October 18, 2013.
- Zambrano, Vincent. "A Conversation with Kim Dorland." *Arte Fuse,* May 25, 2013.

2012

- Campbell, James D. "Kim Dorland, Galerie Division." *Magenta Magazine Online* 3, 1 (February 8, 2012).
- Docimo, Michelina. "Smoking White Hot: Mana Flames the Art Fire." *Culture Catch,* March 13, 2012.
- Hodges, Michael H. "Bright Show Sure Cure for Winter Blahs." *Detroit News,* January 19, 2012.
- Leong, Melissa. "Fresh and for Sale: Contemporary Art Auction Focuses on Art from 1980 to Now." *National Post,* March 6, 2012.

2011

- Angel, Sara. "Kim Dorland: Nocturne." *Eye Weekly,* February 2, 2011.
- Diaz-Berrio, Natalia Lara. "Breaking All the Rules." *The Link,* November 8, 2011.
- Hansen, Michael. "Interview: Kim Dorland." *ArtSync,* January 28, 2011.
- Indrisek, Scott. "Kim Dorland: Painting with Guts." *Modern Painters,* August 24, 2011.
- Jager, David. "Spooky Dorland, New Paintings Go to the Darker Side." *NOW,* January 27, 2011.
- Meier, Allison. "Painting through Your Obsession about Love." *Hyperallergic,* August 23, 2011.
- "Montreal." Paint the Painting (blog), October 28, 2011.
- Morgan, Saretta. "Kim Dorland for Lori." *NY Arts Magazine,* July 21, 2011.
- Pohl, John. "Oil Shows Beauty, Destruction of 'Manufactured Environment,' " *Montreal Gazette*, October 14, 2011.

- "Raw and Unapologetic: Kim Dorland's Portraits of Wife Lori at Mike Weiss Gallery." artdaily.org, July 22, 2011.
- Vaughan, R.M. "Too Toronto-Centric? I Have No Problem with That." *Globe and Mail,* January 1, 2011.
- Zevitas, Steven. "10 Must-See Painting Shows in the US: Summer Heat Edition." *Huffington Post,* July 18, 2011.

2010

- Bahrenburg, Genevieve. "Taxidermy Woodland Animals Dipped in Paint and Sprinkled in Glitter? Yes, See This Exhibit." *Elle,* November 4, 2010.
- Hegert, Natalie. "Eye-Catchers at SCOPE." *ArtSlant,* March 2010.
- ——. "Shack in the Woods." *ArtSlant,* November 14, 2010.
- Intini, John. "That's a Bit Extreme, Isn't It?" *Maclean's,* August 12, 2010.
- Pagel, David. "Kim Dorland at Mark Moore Gallery." *Los Angeles Times,* March 26, 2010.
- Stanton, Chris. "Kim Dorland at Mark Moore Gallery." *Dailydujour,* March 21, 2010.
- Vilas, Amber, and Andrew Russeth. "Scope Comes on Strong." *Artinfo,* March 8, 2010.

2009

- Beem, Edgar Allen. "Home at Westport Arts Center." *Yankee Magazine,* March 31, 2009.
- Catchlove, Lucinda. "Apocalyptic Love." *Zink,* Spring 2009.
- Enright, Robert. "Paint-Wrangler (An Interview with Kim Dorland in Two Parts)." In *Kim Dorland* (catalogue), Bonelli ArteContemporanea.
- Lee, Sasha. "Kim Dorland." *Beautiful/Decay,* June 8, 2009.

- Redfern, Christine. "Artist Uses Big, Gooey Globe." *Montreal Gazette,* April 4, 2009.
- Rosen, Aaron. "Beauty, Phooey." *Artnet Magazine,* June 2009.
- ——. "Bruised Beauty, Paintings by Kim Dorland." *Canadian Art Scene,* June 20, 2009.
- Smith, Roberta. "Kim Dorland: Super! Natural!" *New York Times,* June 19, 2009.
- Sudarsky, Noah Marcel. "Giving Face: Portraits for a New Generation @ Nicholas Robinson Gallery." *Whitehot Magazine,* March 2009.

2008

- *Carte Blanche.* Vol. 2, *Painting.* Toronto: Magenta Publishing for the Arts, 2008.
- Dault, Gary Michael. "Gallery Going." *Globe and Mail,* September 13, 2008.
- Denan, Pierre. *2870 Grams of Art.* Paris: M19.
- Kalm, James. "Kim Dorland *North.*" *Brooklyn Rail,* May 2008.
- *Kim Dorland: The Idea of North* (exhibition catalogue), Freight + Volume, New York.
- "Kim Dorland." *NY Arts,* May–June 2008. www.nyartsmagazine.com/?p=5049.
- Milroy, Sarah. "Curatorial Celebrations? Try Inventor Stockpiles." *Globe and Mail,* November 22, 2008.

2007

- Berry, Melissa. "Where the Grass Is Greener." *FFWD,* September 20, 2007.
- Dault, Gary Michael. "Pigments of the Imagination." *Globe and Mail,* November 10, 2007.
- Doucette, Valerie. "Oil Spill: New Painting in Ontario." *Border Crossings,* 26, 4 (issue 104) (December 2007).

- Goddard, Peter. "Warning: Wet Paint." *Toronto Star,* October 18, 2007.
- Gray, Emma. "Emma Gray's Top 10 Shows in Los Angeles This Month." *Saatchi Online,* November 3, 2007.
- Myers, Holly. "Trailblazing Chinatown Gallery Scene Keeps Up with City's Pace." *Los Angeles Times,* November 11, 2007.
- Tousley, Nancy. "Brush Strokes Expose Angst of Everyday Suburbia." *Calgary Herald,* September 14, 2007.
- Vogl, Rhiannon. "Group of Seven." *Ottawa XPress,* August 9, 2007.

2006

- "Best of Toronto." *NOW,* October 26, 2006.
- Brevi, Manuela. *Into the Woods* (exhibition catalogue), Contemporaneamente, Milan, Italy.
- Dault, Gary Michael. "Gallery Going." *Globe and Mail,* September 15, 2006.
- Hackett, Regina. "Galleries Explore a New World of Landscapes." *Seattle Post-Intelligencer,* June 9, 2006.
- Jager, David. "Dorland's Styles Collide." *NOW,* September 21, 2006.
- ———. "Group Hug at Angell." *NOW,* December 7, 2006.
- McVeigh, Jennifer. "RBC Showcases Canadian Talent." *Calgary Herald,* November 5, 2006.

2005

- Dault, Gary Michael. "Gallery Going." *Globe and Mail,* February 26, 2005.
- ———. "Gallery Going." *Globe and Mail,* December 31, 2005.
- Dault, Julia. "Our Group of Seven." *National Post,* December 8, 2005.
- Goddard, Peter. "Hot Fantasies, Heroes, a Hotel and Much More." *Toronto Star,* February 12, 2005.
- Willard, Christopher. "Losers and Winners: Kim Dorland Homes in on Generation Y." *Calgary Herald,* November 5, 2005.

2004

- Dault, Julia. "Desire, and a Slice of Colour." *National Post,* March 25, 2004.

ACKNOWLEDGEMENTS

THIS BOOK WOULD not have been possible without the generous help and support of many people. Special thanks to Robin Anthony and RBC; Victoria Dickenson, Katerina Atanassova and the McMichael Canadian Art Collection; Jamie Angell, Bruce Bailey, Jim Balsillie and Neve Peric; Paul and Mary Dailey Desmarais III; Belinda Stronach, Petra and Lionel Newton; Megan Long, Brian Cartwright, Robert Enright, Jeffrey Spalding, Eden Robbins, Phil Barker, and Kyle Scheurmann.

The work that makes up this book is dedicated to my two beautiful sons, Seymour and Thomson. And to Lori—I couldn't have done any of this without you. I love you so much.

KIM DORLAND

▲▲ Seymour in the Ernest Avenue studio, Toronto, 2011

▲ With Tommy, Ernest Avenue studio, Toronto, 2011

CONTRIBUTORS

ROBIN ANTHONY is the art curator for the Royal Bank of Canada. She is responsible for the corporate collection and is involved with the RBC Canadian Painting Competition, which supports promising artists in the early stages of their careers. RBC's collection contains more than four thousand original works of art. These paintings, sculptures, works on paper, and photographs are hanging in offices and reception areas across Canada. Prior to her work with RBC, Anthony was a partner in Anthony/Mills Fine Art Services and a fine art advisor.

JEFFREY SPALDING is an artist, writer, and curator. He has served as director at major art museums, including Glenbow Museum (Calgary); University of Lethbridge Art Gallery; Art Gallery of Nova Scotia; and Appleton Museum of Art (Florida). He is the author of numerous books and catalogues. Spalding was president of the Royal Canadian Academy of Arts (2007–10), recipient of the Alberta College of Art and Design Board of Governors Award of Excellence (1992), and awarded the Order of Canada (2007) and the Queen Elizabeth II Diamond Jubilee Medal (2012). Currently, he is artistic director and chief curator at Contemporary Calgary.

KATERINA ATANASSOVA is the chief curator of the McMichael Canadian Art Collection. Since her appointment in 2009, she has led and curated several special exhibitions, among them *The Tree: Form and Substance* (2011) and *You Are Here: Kim Dorland and the Return to Painting* (2013). She was also the co-curator for the enormously successful international touring exhibition *Painting Canada: Tom Thomson and the Group of Seven*. She is a graduate of Sofia University and holds an MA from the Centre for Medieval Studies, University of Toronto. She is currently a PhD candidate at the Department of Art History and Visual Culture at York University, where she is working on urban visuality and the emergence of urban culture in Canada.

ROBERT ENRIGHT is the senior contributing editor and film critic for *Border Crossings* magazine and the University Research Chair in Art Theory and Criticism in the School of Fine Art and Music at the University of Guelph. He is the author of a number of books and has contributed introductions, interviews, and essays to over a hundred books and catalogues. He was a nominator and contributor to both *Vitamin P2* and *Vitamin D2*. In 2005, he was made a member of the Order of Canada. He lives in Winnipeg, Manitoba.

Eastview Sev #2 2010
oil, acrylic, spray paint, copper leaf, and pen
on wood panels, 96 × 216 in.

COLLECTIONS AND PHOTO CREDITS